Monitoring Results for Breeding American Peregrine Falcons (*Falco peregrinus anatum*), 2003

Biological Technical Publication

BTP-R1005-2006

Michael Green[1], Ted Swem[2], Marie Morin[3,11], Robert Mesta[4], Mary Klee[5], Kathy Hollar[6], Rob Hazlewood[7,12], Phil Delphey[8], Robert Currie[9], Michael Amaral[10]

[1] U.S. Fish and Wildlife Service, Region 1, Division of Migratory Birds and Habitat Programs, Portland, OR Michael_green@fws.gov

[2] U.S. Fish and Wildlife Service, Region 7, Ecological Services, Fairbanks, AK

[3] U.S. Fish and Wildlife Service, Region 1, Ecological Services, Portland, OR

[4] Sonoran Joint Venture, Tucson, AZ

[5] U.S. Fish and Wildlife Service, Region 9, Ecological Services, Arlington, VA

[6] U.S. Fish and Wildlife Service, Region 1, Ecological Services, Portland, OR

[7] U.S. Fish and Wildlife Service, Region 6, Ecological Services, Helena, MT

[8] U.S. Fish and Wildlife Service, Region 3, Ecological Services, Bloomington, MN

[9] U.S. Fish and Wildlife Service, Region 4, Ecological Services, Asheville, NC

[10] U.S. Fish and Wildlife Service, Region 5, Ecological Services, Concord, NH

[11] Current address: 4920 SE 140th Ave, Portland, OR 97236

[12] Current address: P.O. Box 4322, Helena, MT 59604

Author Contact information:

Michael Green, U.S. Fish and Wildlife Service, Region 1, Migratory Birds and Habitat Programs, 911 N.E. 11th Ave., Portland, OR 97232-4181. Phone: (503) 872-2707, Fax: (503) 231-2019, E-mail: Michael_Green@fws.gov

Ted Swem, U.S. Fish and Wildlife Service, Fairbanks Fish and Wildlife Office, 101 12th Ave., Box 19, Fairbanks, Alaska 99501. Phone: (907) 456-0441, Fax: (907) 456-0208, E-mail: Ted_Swem@fws.gov.

Marie Morin (Current address), 4920 SE 140th Ave, Portland, Oregon 97236. marie_p_morin@hotmail.com

Robert Mesta, Coordinator, Sonoran Joint Venture, 738 N. Fifth Ave. Suite 215, Tucson, Arizona 85705. Phone: (520) 882-0047, Fax: (520) 882-0370, E-mail: Robert_Mesta@fws.gov.

Mary Klee, U.S. Fish and Wildlife Service, Division of Habitat Conservation Plans, Recovery, and State Grants, 4401 N. Fairfax Dr., Mail Stop 420 Arlington Square, Arlington, VA 22203. Phone: (703) 358-2061, Fax: (703) 358-1735, E-mail: Mary_Klee@fws.gov.

Kathy Hollar, U.S. Fish and Wildlife Service, Region 1, Division of Endangered Species, 911 N.E. 11th Ave., Portland, OR 97232-4181. Phone: (503) 231-2359, Fax: (503) 231-6243, E-mail: Kathy_Hollar@fws.gov.

Robert Hazlewood (Current address), P.O. Box 4322, Helena, MT 59604. Tierra1@theglobal.net

Phil Delphey, U.S. Fish and Wildlife Service, Ecological Services, Twin Cities Field Office, 4101 E. 80th St., Bloomington, Minnesota 55425. Phone: (612) 725-3548, Fax: (612) 725-3609. E-mail: Phil_Delphey@fws.gov.

Robert Currie, U.S. Fish and Wildlife Service, Ecological Services, Asheville Field Office, 160 Zillicoa St., Asheville, North Carolina 28801. Phone: (828) 258-3939, Fax: (828) 258-5330. E-mail: Robert_Currie@fws.gov.

Michael Amaral, U.S. Fish and Wildlife Service, Region 5, Ecological Services, New England Field Office, 70 Commercial St., Ste. 300, Concord, New Hampshire 03301-4986. Phone: (603) 223-2541, Fax: (603) 223-0104, e-mail: Michael_Amaral@fws.gov.

For additional copies or information, contact:
Migratory Birds and Habitat Programs
U.S. Fish and Wildlife Service
911 NE 11th Ave
Portland, OR 97232

Recommended citation:
Green, M.G., T. Swem, M. Morin, R. Mesta, M. Klee, K. Hollar, R. Hazlewood, P. Delphey, R. Currie, and M. Amaral. 2006. Monitoring results for breeding American Peregrine Falcon (*Falco peregrinus anatum*), 2003. U.S. Department of Interior, Fish and Wildlife Service, Biological Technical Publication FWS/BTP-R1005-2006, Washington DC.

Series Senior Technical Editor:
Stephanie L. Jones
USFWS, Region 6
Nongame Migratory Bird Coordinator
P.O. Box 25486
Denver Federal Center
Denver, Colorado 80225-0486

Table of Contents

List of Figures

List of Tables

Acknowledgments

The monitoring team is especially grateful to Bob Steidl for his statistical guidance. However, we would have no data to analyze were it not for more than 300 observers, volunteers and paid personnel, who ventured into the field in 2003 at least two and sometimes many more times over a three to four month period to observe Peregrine Falcons. Territory accessibility ranged from roadside to remote; the latter requiring hiking, rafting, or access by air. This nation-wide monitoring effort by the U.S. Fish and Wildlife Service is completely dependent on the network of State and Federal agencies, Tribes, and many other organizations that marshal this cadre of dedicated observers, annually in many States or regions. The observers themselves, united by their collective dedication to Peregrine Falcons, might not be aware of the larger network to which they belong. We know that Appendix A fails to list all participants and apologize to those overlooked. We hope this list gives some perspective on the number of people involved.

Funding for this effort was provided to States and other cooperators by the U.S. Fish and Wildlife Service. Thanks to George Allen, Brad Bortner, Susan Earnst, Suzanne Fellows, Stephanie L. Jones, Bob Steidl, and Tara Zimmerman for reviewing earlier versions of this report.

Summary

In 2003, the U.S. Fish and Wildlife Service (Service) implemented the first of five nationwide monitoring efforts for American Peregrine Falcons (*Falco peregrinus anatum*) (Peregrine Falcons) as described in the Service's post-delisting monitoring plan (USFWS 2003). More than 300 observers monitored 438 Peregrine Falcon territories across six monitoring regions. Monitoring in the Southwestern monitoring region fell short of the monitoring goal, where 36 of the targeted 96 territories were monitored; efforts are underway to implement full-scale monitoring in that region in 2006. The five other monitoring regions surveyed sufficient territories to meet the statistical criteria described in the post-delisting monitoring plan. Our estimates of territory occupancy, nest success, and productivity were above the target values that we set in the monitoring plan for those nesting parameters. Additional data collected by this effort documented that the total number of nesting pairs of Peregrine Falcons is estimated at 3,005. Additional data show that 92% of pairs nest on natural substrates in all regions except the Midwestern/Northeastern region, where only 32% nest on natural substrates. Our estimates of the nesting parameters and the additional data from across the United States indicate that the Peregrine Falcon population is secure and vital. The next coordinated nationwide monitoring effort is scheduled for 2006 (USFWS 2003).

Introduction

The history of Peregrine Falcons in the United States, their population decline caused by environmental contaminants and their recovery following bans on those chemicals, is a tale of conservation success. By the late 1960's Peregrine Falcons had disappeared from the eastern United States and Midwest and were substantially reduced in the Western United States, Canada, and Mexico (Kiff 1988, Enderson et al. 1995). The Service officially listed Peregrine Falcons as endangered in 1970 under the Endangered Species Conservation Act of 1969, a precursor of the Endangered Species Act (ESA) of 1973 (for a history of listing actions see USFWS 1999) and set recovery goals based on abundance and productivity in four regions of the United States. In some of these regions it also established goals for reduced contaminant effects (USFWS 1982a, 1982b, 1984, 1991, 1993; Figure 1). By 1999, recovery goals had been almost completely met in all regions, primarily due to a ban on the use of DDT and other chlorinated hydrocarbons and to the successful captive breeding, rearing, and release of over 6,000 Peregrine Falcons (White et al. 2002). Peregrine Falcons were removed from the Service's List of Threatened and Endangered Species on August 25, 1999 (USFWS 1999).

From 1999 to 2003 the Service developed a post-delisting monitoring plan (USFWS 2003) for Peregrine Falcons in cooperation with other Federal and State agencies, Tribes, and nongovernmental organizations (USFWS 2003). This plan is designed to detect a significant decline in territory occupancy, nest success, or productivity in six monitoring regions across the United States. These three indices of population health were low between 1950 and 1980 when Peregrine Falcon populations declined severely; the three measures then rebounded during population recovery (Cade et al. 1988, Enderson et al. 1995, USFWS 1999, White et al. 2002). The monitoring plan (USFWS 2003) calls for monitoring every three years beginning in 2003 and ending in 2015. These five monitoring periods meet the requirement of ESA (to monitor ". . . for not less than five years . . .") and the three-year interval spreads the monitoring over 13 years, reflecting the concern of the Service for the long-term future of Peregrine Falcon populations. The monitoring plan is also designed to collect baseline information on contaminant loads in each monitoring region through the annual collection and archiving of addled eggs and feather samples. Those samples will be analyzed and reported in future years. This report is of results from Peregrine Falcon monitoring in 2003, which yielded data on territory occupancy, nest success, and productivity from across the United States. This is the first report of post-delisting monitoring results for Peregrine Falcons.

Methods

Monitoring Regions

The six monitoring regions are: Pacific, Rocky Mountain/Great Plains, Southwestern, Midwestern/Northeastern, Southeastern, and Interior Alaska (Figure 1). The monitoring region boundaries conform to the Service's regional divisions with the exception that Service regions 3 (Great Lakes and Big Rivers) and 5 (Northeast) are combined into a single monitoring region. These monitoring regions are similar to the original four Peregrine Falcon recovery regions, with some minor boundary adjustments (USFWS 2003).

Sample Size Determination

In each of the Pacific, Southwestern, Rocky Mountain/Great Plains, and Midwestern-Northeastern monitoring regions, we randomly selected 96 territories from the set of territories occupied at least once from 1999 through 2002. This is the estimated sample size required to detect a decline in nest success from 68% (average nationwide nest success from 1999-2002) to 55% (potentially indicating an unhealthy population) with a type I error (alpha) of 0.1, and a type II error (beta) less than or equal to 0.2; the statistical power to detect declines of that magnitude is thus greater than or equal to 0.80 (1–beta), or 80% (USFWS 2003). In this effort, power measures the ability of our sampling of the population to accurately reveal the 13 percentage point decline of interest; beta indicates the probability of making a type II statistical error, that is, of incorrectly accepting the null hypothesis that nest success or territory occupancy did not fall by 13 points, when in fact it did. The calculated number of adequately monitored occupied territories to achieve these statistical criteria is 67. The sample size calculation of 96 territories accounts for the fact that Peregrine Falcons occupy about 75% of monitored territories in any year, and a margin of error of 7 (10%) territories per monitoring region to ensure that a sufficient number of nests are monitored. If the initial random selection of territories included a territory that was too difficult to monitor adequately, usually because of inaccessibility, then we randomly selected an alternate from the same pool of territories from the same State. Although this introduces a potential bias to territory selection, we considered it a reasonable way to maintain a sufficient sample in the face of practical considerations of monitoring. Six territories were reselected in this way in 2003.

In the Southeastern Region all known territories ($n = 21$) were monitored. In Interior Alaska, we monitored all territories ($n = 100$) along portions of both the Tanana and Yukon rivers, mostly by boat; these remote stretches of river have been monitored in this way for 20 years, and thus we took advantage of established protocols and manpower to determine the health of Peregrine Falcons in Interior Alaska.

Monitoring Protocol

Peregrine Falcon nest sites were observed by volunteers, agency personnel and other partners (Appendix A). Observers reported data to regional coordinators on a data collection form (Appendix B), who then consolidated the regional monitoring data and sent it to the national coordinator for analysis.

Observers visited each randomly selected territory to determine occupancy, nest success, and productivity. Observers were instructed to maintain sufficient distance from nests so as not to elicit sustained territorial behavior from either adult (Pagel 1992). Occupied territories were those where either a pair of Peregrine Falcons was present (two adults or an adult/subadult mixed pair) or there was evidence of reproduction (e.g., one adult is observed sitting low in the nest, eggs or young are seen, or food is delivered into eyrie). Territories were considered unoccupied if the above criteria were not met after the territory was visited during two observer visits of four or more hours each during the appropriate months (USFWS 2003). The calculation of territory occupancy is the number of occupied territories divided by the number of territories that were monitored.

Nest success is the percentage of occupied territories in a monitoring region with one or more young ≥ 28 days old, with age determined following guidelines in Cade et al. (1996). Productivity is the number of young observed at ≥ 28 days old per occupied territory averaged across a monitoring region (USFWS 2003). Most counts were made of young 28 days old to fledging age (ca. 45 days post-hatch). However, some observers reported the number of young fledged based on visits conducted immediately after fledging. These data were used if they were the only counts of young ≥ 28 days old from that territory. In Interior Alaska, productivity is estimated from observations made during the final transect, regardless of nestling age, although average nestling age is usually between 14 and 28 days.

Some States, Service regions, and private programs monitored all known Peregrine Falcon nesting territories, not just those selected as part of this monitoring effort. Data from these efforts are also summarized here.

Analyses

We compared territory occupancy, nest success, and their 90% confidence intervals, to target values derived from nationwide data collected from 1999 through 2002 (Steidl et al. 1997). These target values are 84% (90% CI = ± 2%) territory occupancy and 68% (90% CI = ± 2%) nest success (USFWS 2003). We also compared the estimates of territory occupancy and nest success and their confidence intervals to "... thresholds for agency response ..." 13 percentage points lower than the target values. The thresholds are 71% for territory occupancy

and 55% for nest success (USFWS 2003). We compared estimates of productivity and their 90% confidence limits to a threshold value of 1.0 nestling per occupied territory; historic, and contemporary productivity; and to estimates of this parameter in Peregrine Falcon population models (USFWS 2003). We used the finite population correction in our calculations of confidence intervals around estimates of territory occupancy, nest success, and productivity (Scheaffer et al. 1996). The finite population correction requires knowledge of the overall population size. For Peregrine Falcons, we are fairly confident in our estimate of overall population size in each region. Regardless, we made the conservative assumption that the total nesting population was 10% larger in each region than is currently known, perhaps more likely in Western than in Midwestern, Eastern, or Southern regions.

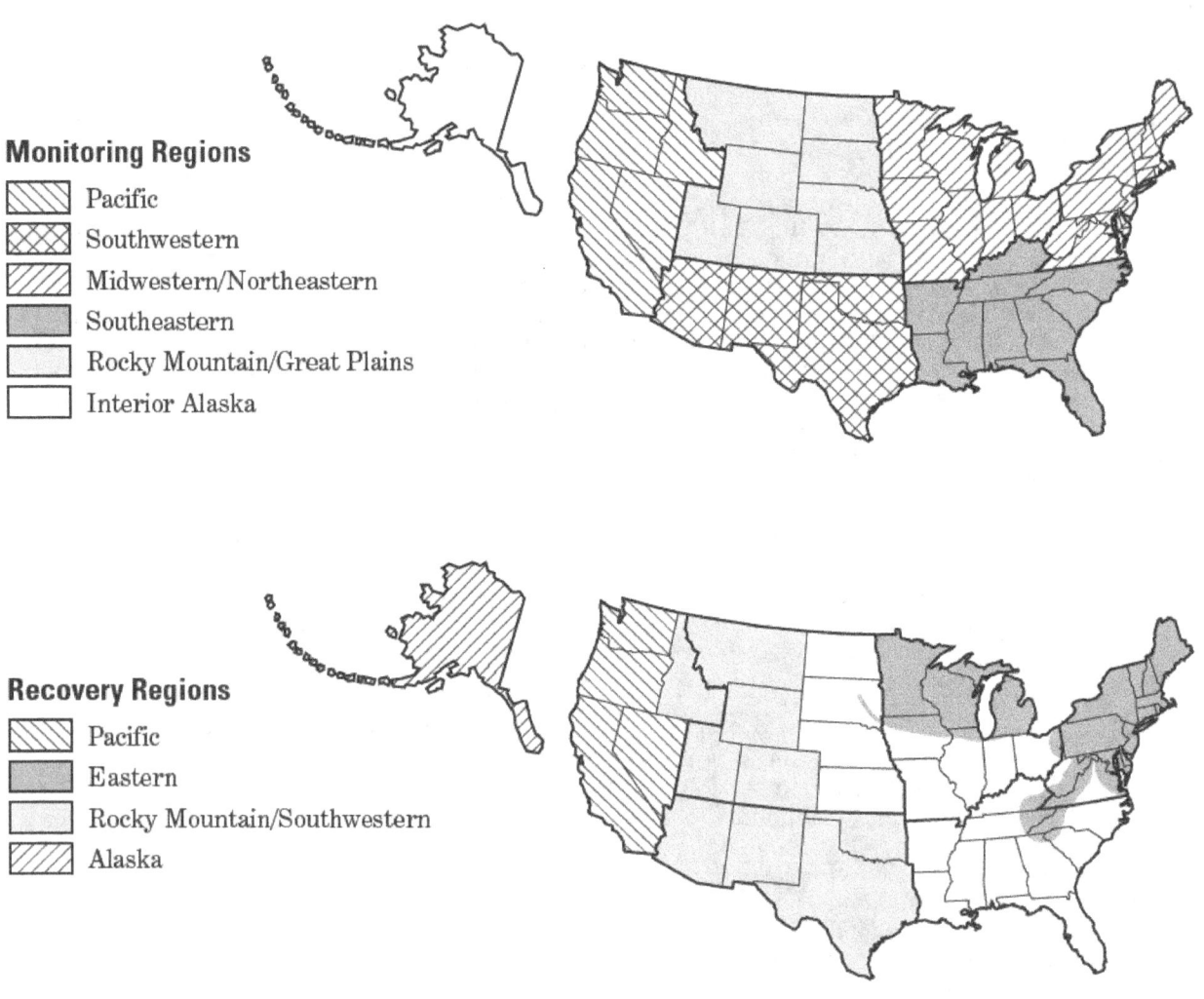

Figure 1: Monitoring and recovery regions for the American Peregrine Falcon, 2003. Service Region boundaries outlined in each map—Region 1 (Pacific, excluding Hawaii and other Pacific Islands); R2 (Southwest); R3 (Great Lakes-Big Rivers); R4 (Southeast, excluding Puerto Rico & Virgin Islands); R5 (Northeast); R6 (Mountain-Prairie); R7 (Alaska).

Results

Across the nation, 438 Peregrine Falcon territories were monitored (Table 1; Appendix C): 36 in the Southwestern Region (New Mexico and Big Bend National Park, TX); 21 in the Southeastern Region; 100 in Interior Alaska; 96 in the Pacific Region; 95 in the Midwestern/Northeastern Region; and 90 in the Rocky Mountain/Great Plains Region. Some territories were incompletely monitored and were omitted from further analysis. Regardless, sample sizes were sufficient to achieve the statistical targets of the monitoring plan for all monitoring regions except the Southwestern Region (Table 1). In the Southwestern Region, the power to detect 13 point declines in nest success and territory occupancy dropped to 53% and 63%, respectively, due to limited sample sizes.

Estimates of territory occupancy varied from 78% to 95% across regions and averaged 87% for the nation (Table 2). Ninety percent confidence intervals around their means included or exceeded the target value of 84% (Figure 2). In the Southwestern Region the estimated territory occupancy was 78%; the 90% confidence interval (67% to 89%) included the threshold for Service response for territory occupancy, which is 71%, 13 points lower than the target of 84% (USFWS 2003).

Estimates of nest success ranged from 64% to 78% across regions and averaged 71% for the nation (Table 2). Ninety percent confidence limits around nest success means included or exceeded the 68% target value, and were all above the threshold for agency response (Figure 2).

Estimates of productivity varied from 1.45–2.09 across regions and averaged 1.64 for the nation (Table 2), and 90% confidence intervals exceeded the threshold for agency response of 1.0 (Figure 2).

In the Southeastern Region observers monitor every known territory. Thus, the summarized data from this region likely represent true values for southeastern Peregrine Falcons rather than estimates of those values as in other regions. Nevertheless, we assumed there are a few territories that have not been discovered and thus also show confidence intervals around the 'estimates' of the population parameters in the Southeast.

Data beyond that requested in the Monitoring Plan were reported by States or monitoring regions, including the number of newly discovered territories in 2003, updated counts of occupied territories, and the number of pairs using manmade structures

Table 1: Territory and nest data, American Peregrine Falcon, 2003.

Region	Territories Checked	Territories Occupied (known outcome)[1]	Successful Nests[2]	Number of Young[3]
Pacific	96	80 (75)	49	109
Southwestern	36	28 (26)	20	45
Midwestern/Northeastern	95	86 (82)	62	171
Southeastern	21	20 (18)	14	28
Rocky Mountain/Great Plains	90	78 (70)	52	104
Interior Alaska	100	89 (89)	57	133
All Regions	438	381 (360)	254	590

[1] Some territories were excluded from nest success and productivity calculations because they were not checked when nestlings were ≥28 days old, and thus the outcome was considered unknown.

[2] Includes only territories with young ≥28 days old.

[3] Maximum number of nestlings ≥28 days old detected on last visit to nest, or count of fledged young if the only nest visit after 27 days post-hatch was made after young fledged.

versus natural. Using this information, the estimated number of Peregrine Falcon territories in North America in 2003 was conservatively estimated at 3005, including recent data from Canada (400 pairs; U. Banasch, pers. commun.), an older estimate from Mexico (170 pairs; Enderson et al. 1995), and a rough estimate for Interior Alaska (1000 pairs; T. Swem, pers. commun.). In the contiguous United States, the total number of active territories was estimated to be 1435 (Table 3).

Of the 438 territories checked, 350 were on natural substrates and 88 were on manmade structures (Table 4). Artificial substrates supported 64% of eyries in the Midwestern/Northeastern region, but only 8% of nests in all other regions combined (Figure 3).

Table 2: Territory occupancy, nest success, and productivity for the American Peregrine Falcon, 2003.

Region	% Territory Occupancy[1] (90% CI)	% Nest Success[2] (90% CI)	Productivity[3] (90% CI)
Pacific	83 (78–89)	65 (57–74)	1.45 (1.25-1.66)
Southwestern	78 (67–89)	77 (64–90)	1.73 (1.36-2.10)
Midwestern/Northeastern	91 (86–95)	76 (69–82)	2.09 (1.85-2.32)
Southeastern	95 (93–98)	78 (70–86)	1.56 (1.32-1.79)
Rocky Mountain/Great Plains	87 (81–92)	74 (66–82)	1.49 (1.29-1.68)
Interior Alaska	89 (84–94)	64 (56–72)	1.49[4] (1.27-1.72)
All Regions	87 (85–89)	71 (67–74)	1.64 (1.53-1.75)

[1] Percent of checked territories occupied by a pair.

[2] Percent of occupied territories with one or more young ≥28 days old.

[3] Average number of young ≥28 days old produced by occupied territories with known outcomes.

[4] Average age of young was 14 days on Yukon and 21-28 days on Tanana rivers, thus productivity estimates are unlike in other regions. In a previous year on Yukon, a count of nestlings and later of fledglings of a sample of nests yielded a 21% mortality rate (Skip Ambrose, pers. comm.). If applied to both rivers, this mortality correction would result in a productivity estimate of 1.18 (90% CI 0.95-1.41); however, this calculation is also not equivalent to our method of estimating productivity in other regions.

Table 3: 2003 continental population estimate, American Peregrine Falcon.

Region	Pairs (new[1])	Total
Pacific	472 (87)	
Rocky Mountain/Great Plains	367 (10)	
Southwestern	260 (0)	1099 (97)
Midwestern/Northeastern	315 (24)	
Southeastern	21 (2)	336 (26)
Subtotal (lower 48)		1435 (123)
Interior Alaska	1000 (8)	
Canada	400	
Mexico	170	
Total[2]	3005 (131)	

[1]Number of new territories reported in 2003 versus 2002; in some cases these updated older data (5 year-old data in one case).

[2]Includes conservative estimates for some States (e.g. CA, AK) where exact pair count not known.

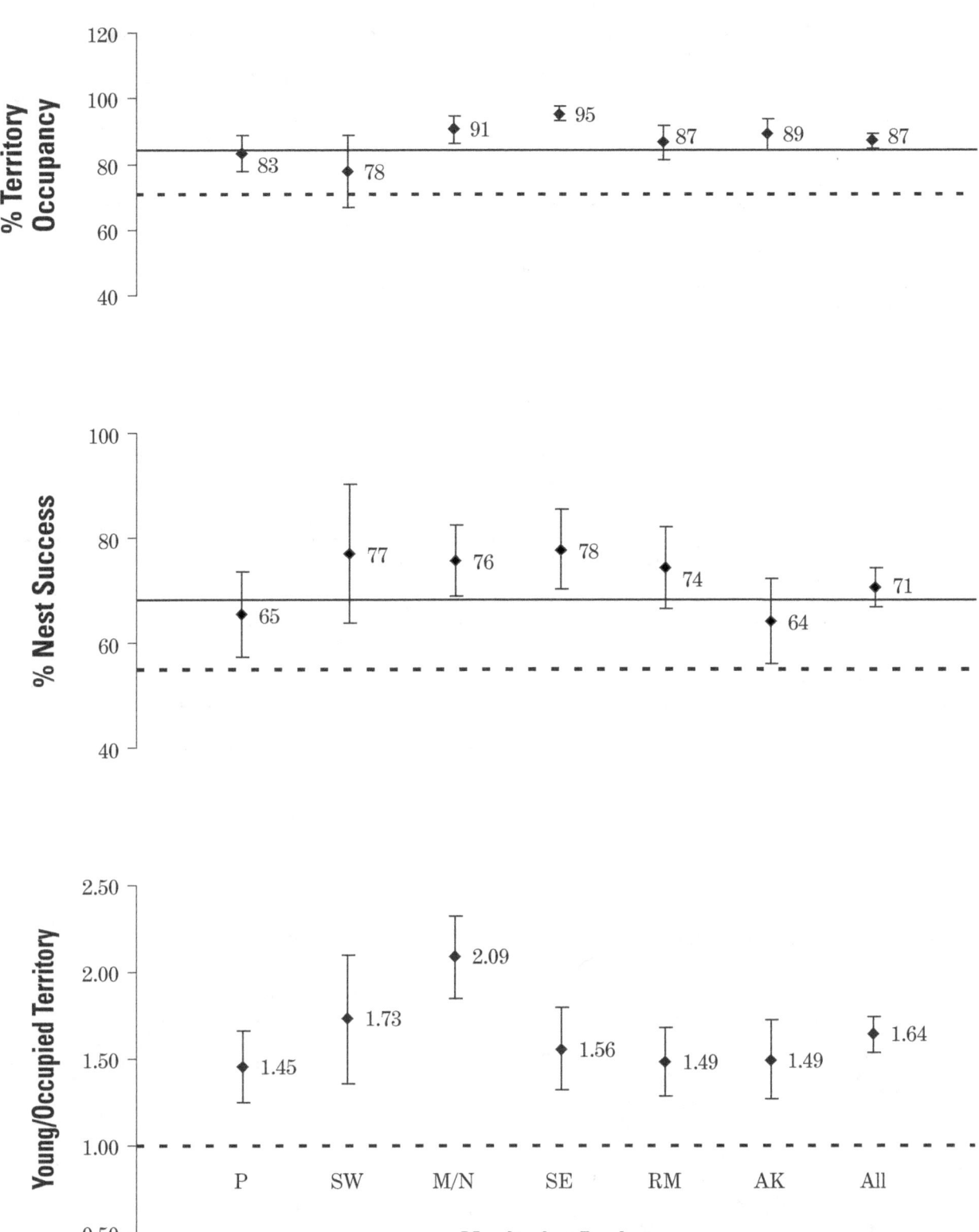

Figure 2: American Peregrine Falcon, 2003, regional estimates of territory occupancy, nest success, productivity, and 90% confidence intervals. Target values (solid lines at 84% territory occupancy and 68% nest success), and threshold levels (dashed lines at 71% territory occupancy, 55% nest success, and 1.0 Productivity). Monitoring Regions are: P, Pacific; SW, Southwestern; M/N, Midwestern/Northeastern; SE, Southeastern; RM, Rocky Mountain/Great Plains; AK, Interior Alaska; and combined data for all regions.

Table 4: Numbers of nest sites on natural versus manmade substrates, American Peregrine Falcon, 2003.

Regions	Nest Site Substrate	Territories Checked	Territories Occupied (known outcome)	Successful Nests	Young
Pacific	Manmade	15	14 (14)	8	21
	Natural	81	66 (61)	41	88
Southwestern	Manmade	0	0	0	0
	Natural	36	28 (26)	20	45
Midwestern/ Northeastern	Manmade	61	58 (57)	45	132
	Natural	34	28 (25)	17	39
Southeastern	Manmade	8	7 (7)	7	13
	Natural	13	13 (11)	7	15
Rocky Mountain/ Great Plains	Manmade	4	3 (3)	2	3
	Natural	86	75 (67)	50	101
Interior Alaska	Manmade	0	0	0	0
	Natural	100	89 (89)	57	133
All Regions	Manmade	88	82 (81)	62	169
	Natural	350	299 (279)	192	421
Total		438	381 (360)	254	590

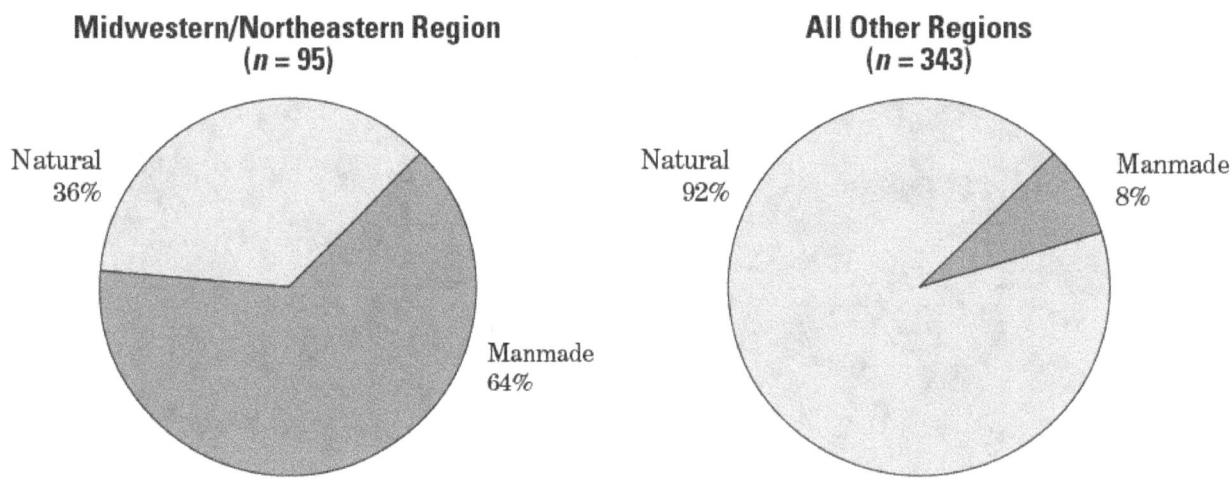

Figure 3: Percentage of eyries on natural versus manmade substrates in the Midwestern/Northeastern Monitoring Region and all other regions combined, American Peregrine Falcon, 2003.

Discussion

The Monitoring Plan describes three conditions that might cause concern about Peregrine Falcons in a region or regions and lead to additional action by the Service. The three conditions are: estimates of territory occupancy or nest success at or below the thresholds for agency response, that is, 13 percentage points below the 1999–2002 targets; or if the upper bound of the 90% confidence intervals around those estimates are below the 1999–2002 targets; or if estimates of productivity are below 1.0 young per successful territory. These thresholds were based on data thought to represent healthy Peregrine Falcon populations (Hickey 1942, Hickey and Anderson 1969, Enderson and Craig 1974, Ratcliffe 1993, Hunt 1998, Corser et al. 1999, Hayes and Buchanan 2002). In 2003, none of these conditions was met (Table 2; Figure 2), giving us reasonable confidence that Peregrine Falcons continued to thrive in 2003.

In the Southwestern region, however, the confidence interval for territory occupancy (67% to 89%) is particularly wide; it included the threshold for agency response (71%) (Figure 2); this was a result not considered in the Monitoring Plan. This simply means that territory occupancy may be at or below the threshold for agency response. The wide confidence interval is due in part to the small sample ($n = 36$), 60 fewer, all in Arizona, than our goal of 96 territories per region. Unlike most other states, Arizona discontinued monitoring in 1997 when the number of active territories in the State approached 170 (USFWS 1993); this number far exceeded the goal in the recovery plan of 46 territories for Arizona (USFWS 1984) and approached the 183 territory recovery goal for the entire Rocky Mountain/Southwestern recovery region. Re-establishing the network of volunteers and agency contacts necessary to carry out monitoring in 2003 and compiling an updated list of recently occupied territories was difficult. These and other factors contributed to the shortfall of territories in the Southwestern Region. In 2004 and 2005 territories were re-located throughout Arizona. Sixty of these will be monitored in 2006, increasing our Southwestern sample to 96, and thus achieving our monitoring objectives for statistical power in the Southwestern region.

Although it is not the intent of the Monitoring Plan to track the total numbers of breeding Peregrine Falcons in any region, the monitoring effort does incidentally reveal new territories. The estimate of 3005 pairs in North America is similar to the 2500–3000 pairs estimated in White et al. (2002). Reporting of these data was not universal, however, so the regional and North American sums should be considered conservative estimates.

Data on nest placement were also additional to the main purpose of the monitoring plan. It is not surprising that the majority of nesting pairs in the Midwestern/Northeastern Region selected manmade structures for their eyries; steep, tall cliff faces, classical Peregrine Falcon nesting sites, are fewer in the Midwest than in Western or some Northeastern States. Nonetheless, Peregrine Falcons thrive on smokestacks, tall structures in cities, and on bridges over rivers in this region, where territory occupancy, nest success, and productivity are among the highest in the nation (Table 2). In 13 Midwestern states, Ontario, and Manitoba, productivity from nests on smokestacks and buildings was higher than on cliffs or bridges (Tordoff et al. 2003).

Conclusion

The Monitoring Plan was carried out with few complications at the national level. The sample from the Southwestern region was smaller than recommended, however steps were taken in 2004 and 2005 to prepare for full-scale monitoring in 2006. With the caveat that the Southwestern region was under-sampled, the data collected in 2003 show territory occupancy, nest success, and productivity of Peregrine Falcons to be at healthy levels in every monitoring region, and show numbers of pairs continuing to increase across the United States. No additional reviews or requests for additional research or monitoring occurred as a result of these data. Monitoring will be conducted again in 2006 in accordance with the monitoring plan (USFWS 2003), and funding has already been received by regional coordinators to ensure that States and other partners receive timely support in advance of the 2006 field season to carry out their monitoring activities in accord with the monitoring plan (USFWS 2003).

Literature Cited

Cade, T. J., J. H. Enderson, and J. Linthicum. 1996. Guide to management of Peregrine Falcons at the eyrie. The Peregrine Fund, Boise, ID.

Cade, T. J., J. H. Enderson, C. G. Thelander, and C. M. White, eds. 1988. Peregrine Falcon populations; their management and recovery. The Peregrine Fund, Boise, ID.

Corser, J. D., M. Amaral, C. J. Martin, and C.C. Rimmer. 1999. Recovery of a cliff-nesting Peregrine Falcon, *Falco peregrinus*, population in northern New York and New England, 1984-1996. Canadian Field-Naturalist 113:472-480.

Enderson, J. H., and J. Craig. 1974. Status of the Peregrine Falcon in the Rocky Mountains in 1973. Auk 91:727-736.

Enderson, J. H., W. Heinrich, L. Kiff, and C. M. White. 1995. Population changes in North American Peregrines. Transactions of the 60th North American Wildlife and Natural Resources Conference 1995:142-161.

Hayes, G. E., and J. B. Buchanan. 2002. Washington State status report for the Peregrine Falcon. Washington Department of Fish and Wildlife, Olympia, WA.

Hickey, J. J. 1942. Eastern population of the Duck Hawk. Auk 59:176-204.

Hickey, J. J., and D. W. Anderson. 1969. The Peregrine Falcon: life history and population literature, p. 3-42. *In* J. J. Hickey [ed.], Peregrine Falcon populations: their biology and decline. University of Wisconsin Press, Madison, WI.

Hunt. W. G. 1998. Raptor floaters at Moffat's equilibrium. Oikos 82:191-197.

Kiff, L. F. 1988. Commentary—Changes in the status of the Peregrine in North America: an overview, p. 123-139. *In* T. J. Cade, J. H. Enderson, C. G. Thelander, and C. M. White [eds.], Peregrine Falcon populations: their management and recovery. The Peregrine Fund, Boise, ID.

Pagel, J. E. 1992. Protocol for observing known and potential Peregrine Falcon eyries in the Pacific Northwest, p. 83-96. *In* J. E. Pagel [ed.]. Proceedings: Symposium on Peregrine Falcons in the Pacific Northwest. Administrative Report, Rogue River National Forest, Medford, OR.

Ratcliffe, D. 1993. The Peregrine Falcon, Second edition. T. & A. D. Poyser, London.

Scheaffer, R. L., W. Mendenhall III, and R. L. Ott. 1996. Elementary Survey Sampling, 5th ed. Duxbury Press, Boston, MA.

Steidl, R. J., J. P. Hayes, and E. Schauber. 1997. Statistical power in wildlife research. Journal of Wildlife Management 61:270-279.

Tordoff, H. B, J. A. Goggin, and J. S. Castrale. 2003. Midwest Peregrine Falcon restoration, 2003 annual report. Museum of Natural History, University of Minnesota, Minneapolis, MN.

U.S. Fish and Wildlife Service. 1982a. Pacific Coast recovery plan for the American Peregrine Falcon (*Falco peregrinus anatum*). U.S. Fish and Wildlife Service, Portland, OR.

U.S. Fish and Wildlife Service. 1982b. Recovery plan for the Peregrine Falcon, Alaska population. U.S. Fish and Wildlife Service, Anchorage, AK.

U.S. Fish and Wildlife Service. 1984. American Peregrine Falcon Rocky Mountain population recovery plan. U.S. Fish and Wildlife Service, Denver, CO.

U.S. Fish and Wildlife Service. 1991. Peregrine Falcon (*Falco peregrinus*) eastern population revised recovery plan. U.S. Fish and Wildlife Service, Hadley, MA.

U.S. Fish and Wildlife Service. 1993. American Peregrine Falcon (Western States) (*Falco peregrinus anatum*): addendum to the Pacific Coast (1982) and Rocky Mountain/Southwest (revised, 1984) American Peregrine Falcon recovery plans. U.S. Fish and Wildlife Service, Portland, OR.

U.S. Fish and Wildlife Service. 1999. Endangered
and threatened wildlife and plants; final rule to
remove the American Peregrine Falcon from
the Federal list of endangered and threatened
wildlife, and to remove the similarity of
appearance provision for free-flying peregrines in
the conterminous United States. U.S. DOI., U.S.
Fish and Wildlife Service. Federal Register 64:
46542-46558.

U.S. Fish and Wildlife Service. 2003. Monitoring
plan for the American Peregrine Falcon, A species
recovered under the Endangered Species Act.
U.S. Fish and Wildlife Service, Divisions of
Endangered Species and Migratory Birds and
State Programs, Pacific Region, Portland, OR.

White, C. M., N. J. Clum, T. J. Cade, and W. G. Hunt.
2002. Peregrine Falcon (*Falco peregrinus*). *In*
A. Poole and F. Gill, editors. The birds of North
America, No. 660. The Academy of Natural
Sciences, Philadelphia, Pennsylvania; The
American Ornithologists' Union, Washington,
D.C.

Appendix A: List of Data Collectors by Monitoring Region and State

Pacific Region

California: Paul Andreano, Doug Bell, Dave Bogener, John Boyd, Jeb Bridges, Kristi Bridges, Roy Burke, Ken Dexter, Gregg Doney, Sandra Fleming, Jerry Franklin, Dennis Garrison, Larry Goldzband, David Gregoire, Bill Grummer, Gary Guliasi, Jim Hallisey, Keith Hamm, Terry Hunt, Bob Isenberg, Josh Koepke, Christopher Kuntzsch, Brian Latta, Janet Linthicum, Jeff Maurer, David Moore, Laura Nelson-Bradley, Henry Pontarelli, Richard Rowlette, Andrew Santa Cruz, Christy Sherr, Steve Shubert, Jeff Sipple, Glenn Stewart, David Suddjian, Nick Todd, Brian Walton.

Idaho: Brian Aber, Carl Anderson, Bill Arnold, Mike Biggs, Joanne Bonn, Michael Boyles, Rita Dixon, Robin Garwood, Bruce Haak, Lauri Hanauska-Brown, Kristin Hassalblad, Jim Johnston, Jim Juza, Ed Levine, Alvin McCollough, Julie Mulholland, Greg Painter, Dave Roberts, Hadley Roberts, Rex Sallabanks, Audra Serrian, Dave Spicer, Beth Waterbury, Rick Weaver.

Nevada: Pat Cummings, Bob Furtek, Ross Haley, Kris Kenney, Christy Klinger, Sara McFarland, Julien Peligrini, Vaughan Spearman, Cris Tomlinson, Jason Williams,

Oregon: Ken Allison, David Anderson, Ralph Anderson, Janet Anthony, Norm Barrett, Jean Battle, Matteo Bianchi, Gary Birch, Jeff Bohler, Laura Bradley, Cindy Bright, Bonnie Brown, Matt Broyles, Charlie Bruce, Tim Burnett, Steve Burns, Todd Bush, Francesca Cafferata, Doug Calvin, Steve Carter, Gary Clowers, Kevin Crowell, Eric Cummings, Dick Davis, Ray Davis, Marilyn Elston, Kendel Emmerson, Bus Engsberg, Delena Engsberg, Ron Escano, Roli Espinosa, Sharnelle Fee, Bev Fenske, Dan Fenske, Kim Garvey, Elizabeth Gayner, Lynn Gemlo, Damon Goodman, Eric Greenquist, Bob Gritsky, Lori Haack, Jim Harper, Jim Heaney, Jaime Heinzelmann, Mark Henjum, Will High, Kelli Hoffman, Cindy Humphreys, Frank Isaacs, Kimberly Judson, Shane Kamrath, Anthony Kerwin, Kevin Kocarek, Anson Koehler, Tuch Korevia, Rod Krahmer, Katrina Krause, Karen Kronner, Kirk Lunstrum, Bill Marshall, Jay Martini, Nathan Maxon, Chad McLane, Tom Meek, Michael Mefford, Rolando Mendez-Treneman, Mike Miller, John Moore, Raul Morales, Gail Morris, Reed Mortenson, Bill Munro, Tom Murtagh, Jane Olson, Charlotte Opp, Ralph Opp, Joel Pagel, Rosa Palarino, Amanda Pantovich, Dan Patterson, Mark Penninger, Lindsey Perrine, Dave Peterson, Summer Phelps, Glenn Phillips, Dave Pitkin, Kristal Plotts, Bill Price, Jim Quincy, Erich Reeder, Rick Rodriguez, Trisha Roninger, Bob Sallinger, Jennifer Sanborn, Kevin Sands, Ruby Seitz, Hud Sherlock, Jean Sherlock, Ryan Siebdrath, Devin Simmons, Melonie Smeltz, Jeff Stephens, Terri Stone, Kristin Thompson, Melinda Trask, Sally Villegas, Angie Voigt, Eugene Voyton, Daryl Whitmore, Grant Wiegert, Holly Witt, Barbara Woodhouse, John Woodhouse, Tiff Young.

Washington: Chris Addison, Bud Anderson, David Anderson, Jeff Bernatowicz, Russ Canniff, Tom Cyra, Bob Davies, Howard Ferguson, Pat Fowler, Steve Goodman, Stuart Johnson, Lee Kantar, Michael MacDonald, Tom McCall, Ruth Milner, Kim Romain-Bondi, Tricia Thompson, Dave Volsen.

Southwestern Region

New Mexico: Sandy Williams

Texas: Judy Brinkerhoff, Jessica Erickson, Joselyn Fenstermacher, Allison Freeman, Meaghan Hicks, Katrina Jensen, Dan Leavitt, Gary Luce, Steve McAllister, Colm Moore, Amy Mowat, Marcos Paredes, Casey Parks, Melissa Powell, Michael Ryan, Joe Sirotnak, Raymond Skiles, Reine Winote, David Yim, Mark Yuhas.

Midwestern/Northeastern

Connecticut: Julie Victoria.

Delaware: Holly Niederriter.

Iowa: Theresa Chapel, Pat Schlarbaum

Illinois: Matt Gies, Mary Hennen, Kanae Hirabayashi, Dave Sysczak, Friends of the Uptown Theatre.

Indiana: Susan Banta, Dwayne Burke, John Castrale, Greg Costakis, Tony DiPaolo, Susan Laflin, John Meyer, Jeff Neumeier, Ted Weitzel, John Winebrenner, Wayne Yoder.

Maine: Charlie Todd.

Maryland: Craig Koppie.

Massachusetts: Tom French.

Michigan: Tim Payne, Ray Rustem, Judy Yerkey.

Minnesota: Bob Anderson, Jim Fitzpatrick, Brad
Johnson, Warren Lind, Marco Restani, Wendell
Snider, Bud Tordoff.

New Hampshire: John Kanter, Chris Martin.

New Jersey: Kathy Clark.

New York: Barbara Loucks, Chris Nadareski.

Ohio: Tom Henry, Rick Jasper, Dave Scott.

Pennsylvania: Dan Brauning.

Virginia: Jeff Cooper, Rick Reynolds, Bryan Watt.

Vermont: Doug Blodgett, Steve Faccio,
Margaret Fowle.

Wisconsin: Mike Crivello, Greg Septon.

Southeastern

Georgia: Jim Ozier.

Kentucky: Shawchyi Vorisek.

North Carolina: Chris McGrath.

South Carolina: Mary Bunch, Harrison.

Tennessee: Dubke, Stiver, Keith Watson.

Rocky Mountain/Great Plains

Colorado: Jerry Craig, Jim Enderson, Jeff Lucas,
Terry Meyers, Dinosaur National Monument,
Mark Roberts, Marni Zaborac.

Montana: Byron Crow, David Lockman, Ralph
Rogers, Jay Sumner.

Utah: Frank Howe.

Wyoming: Terry McEneaney, Bob Oakleaf,
Susan Patla.

Interior Alaska

Skip Ambrose, Peter Bente, Bob Ritchie,
John Wright.

We apologize to anyone we left off the list.

Appendix B: Sample Peregrine Falcon Monitoring Form

(Used in 2003; updated version at http://www.fws.gov/endangered/recovery/peregrine/.)

Observation Date:(M/D/YR) _____   Nest Site Name or #_____

Which Territory Visit is this? (circle one)   1st   2nd   3rd   4th

Nest Site (circle one):   Manmade   Natural

Observation Time: Begin _____ End _____

(Should be at least 4 hrs if occupancy, nest age, or nestling number are in question)

Observer(s) _____

Phone:_____ Email:_____ Agency/NGO _____

WEATHER: Precipitation _____ Wind (speed estimate) _____

Temperature _____ Cloud cover (%) _____

Note conditions at beginning (beg.) and ending (end) of observation period if different

Observation post: (distance in meters) _____

Approx. Nesting Phase (determined how?) _____

_____

Peregrines present: (define as ad. male, ad. female, ad. unknown, subad. Male, subad. Female, or subad.

Unknown, and number of each.) _____

Behaviors observed: _____

_____

_____

Nest observed? Y N   Feeding at nest observed? Y N   Eggs observed? Y N Unk

How many eggs? _____ Young observed (AGE)? _____

How many young? Other observations: _____

_____

_____

Occupied Territory—a territory where either a pair of Peregrines are present (2 adults or adult/subadult mixed pair), or there is evidence of reproduction (e.g., one adult is observed sitting low in the nest, eggs or young are seen, or food is delivered into eyrie). Occupancy must be established for at least one of two or more 4-hour site visits. *Nest Success*—the percentage of occupied territories in which one or more young ≥28 days old is observed, with age determined following guidelines in Cade et al. (1996). *Productivity*—the number of young observed (at ≥28 days old) per occupied territory, averaged across the monitoring region.

Appendix C: Monitoring Data

Table C-1: Monitoring Data

FWS ID	Nest Substrate[1]	Occupied?[1]	Adult/Subadult[1]	Successful?[1]	Young[1]
Pacific Monitoring Region					
CA-01	nat	Y	2/0	Y	2
CA-02	nat	Y	2/0	N	0
CA-04	nat	Y	2/0	Y	2
CA-10	nat	Y	2/0	Y	1
CA-11	nat	Y	2/0	Y	4
CA-14	nat	Y	2/0	N	0
CA-15	nat	Y	2/0	unk	unk
CA-21	nat	Y	2/0	Y	3
CA-23	nat	Y	2/0	unk	unk
CA-26	nat	Y	2/0	Y	1
CA-27	nat	Y	2/0	Y	3
CA-31	mm	Y	2/0	Y	1
CA-32	mm	Y	2/0	Y	2
CA-46	nat	Y	2/0	N	0
CA-48	nat	N	0	N	0
CA-54	nat	N	0	N	0
CA-56	nat	Y	2/0	Y	1
CA-62	nat	Y	2/0	N	0
CA-63	nat	Y	2/0	Y	2
CA-64	nat	Y	2/0	Y	2
CA-66	mm	Y	2/0	Y	4
CA-75	mm	Y	2/0	N	0
CA-78	mm	Y	2/0	N	0
CA-82	mm	Y	2/0	Y	2
CA-84	nat	Y	2/0	unk	unk
CA-85	nat	Y	2/0	Y	1
CA-88	nat	Y	2/0	Y	2
CA-89	nat	Y	2/0	Y	2
CA-90	nat	Y	2/0	Y	2
CA-17	nat	Y	2/0	unk	unk
ID-03	nat	Y	2/0	N	0
ID-07	mm	Y	2/0	Y	4

1–*Nest Substrate* (s) are nat (natural, e.g. cliffs) or mm (manmade, e.g. bridges and buildings). *Occupied* and *Successful* nests either Y = Yes or N = No (definitions in Methods). Adult/Subadult often not recorded, thus one number appears. Number of *Young* listed, or unk if last visit was made with young <28 d old.

FWS ID	Nest Substrate[1]	Occupied?[1]	Adult/Subadult[1]	Successful?[1]	Young[1]
ID-09	nat	Y	2/0	Y	3
ID-11	nat	Y	2/0	Y	2
ID-12	nat	N	0	N	0
ID-16	nat	N	0	N	0
ID-17	nat	Y	2/0	N	0
ID-20	nat	Y	2/0	Y	2
ID-24	nat	Y	2/0	Y	1
NV-01	nat	Y	2/0	unk	unk
NV-04	nat	N	1/0	N	0
NV-11	nat	Y	2/0	Y	1
OR-01	nat	Y	2/0	N	0
OR-05	nat	N	1/0	N	0
OR-07	mm	Y	2/0	Y	4
OR-10	nat	N	0	N	0
OR-13	nat	N	1/0	N	0
OR-14	nat	Y	2/0	Y	2
OR-15	nat	Y	2/0	Y	3
OR-21	nat	Y	2/0	N	0
OR-22	mm	Y	2/0	Y	1
OR-23	nat	Y	2/0	N	0
OR-30	nat	Y	2/0	Y	2
OR-31	nat	Y	2/0	Y	3
OR-39	nat	N	0	N	0
OR-41	mm	N	0	N	0
OR-47	nat	Y	2/0	Y	3
OR-49	nat	Y	2/0	N	0
OR-53	nat	Y	2/0	Y	1
OR-56	nat	Y	2/0	N	0
OR-57	nat	Y	2/0	N	0
OR-62	nat	Y	2/0	N	0
OR-63	nat	Y	2/0	Y	3
OR-68	nat	Y	2/0	Y	4
OR-71	nat	N	1/0	N	0
OR-72	mm	Y	2/0	Y	3
OR-75	nat	Y	2/0	Y	3
OR-77	nat	Y	2/0	Y	2
OR-79	nat	N	1/0	N	0
OR-84	nat	Y	2/0	N	0
OR-86	nat	Y	2/0	N	0
OR-90	nat	Y	2/0	Y	2
WA-03	nat	Y	?	Y	2
WA-13	nat	Y	?	Y	3
WA-15	nat	Y	2/0	N	0

1–*Nest Substrate* (s) are nat (natural, e.g. cliffs) or mm (manmade, e.g. bridges and buildings). *Occupied* and *Successful* nests either Y = Yes or N = No (definitions in Methods). Adult/Subadult often not recorded, thus one number appears. Number of *Young* listed, or unk if last visit was made with young <28 d old.

FWS ID	Nest Substrate[1]	Occupied?[1]	Adult/Subadult[1]	Successful?[1]	Young[1]
WA-20	nat	Y	2/0	Y	2
WA-22	nat	Y	?	Y	2
WA-24	nat	Y	2/0	N	0
WA-25	nat	N	0	N	0
WA-29	nat	Y	2/0	Y	1
WA-32	nat	Y	2/0	Y	4
WA-36	mm	Y	2/0	N	0
WA-39	nat	N	1/0	N	0
WA-41	nat	N	0	N	0
WA-47	mm	Y	2/0	N	0
WA-51	nat	Y	2/0	N	0
WA-53	nat	Y	2/0	Y	1
WA-54	nat	Y	2/0	N	0
WA-57	nat	Y	2/0	N	0
WA-60	mm	Y	1/0	N	0
WA-62	nat	Y	2/0	Y	3
WA-63	nat	Y	?	Y	2
WA-74	mm	Y	?	N	0
WA-77	nat	N	0	N	0
WA-79	nat	Y	2/0	Y	2
WA-80	nat	Y	2/0	Y	1

Southwestern Monitoring Region

FWS ID	Nest Substrate[1]	Occupied?[1]	Adult/Subadult[1]	Successful?[1]	Young[1]
NM-004	nat	Y	2/0	Y	1
NM-005	nat	Y	2/0	unk	unk
NM-007	nat	N	1/0	N	0
NM-010	nat	Y	2/0	Y	2
NM-011	nat	Y	2/0	Y	3
NM-013	nat	Y	2/0	Y	2
NM-016	nat	Y	2/0	N	0
NM-021	nat	N	0	N	0
NM-026	nat	Y	2/0	Y	2
NM-029	nat	Y	2/0	Y	2
NM-038	nat	N	0	N	0
NM-040	nat	Y	2/0	Y	1
NM-041	nat	Y	2/0	Y	2
NM-042	nat	N	0	N	0
NM-046	nat	Y	2/0	N	0
NM-050	nat	N	0	N	0
NM-055	nat	Y	2/0	Y	2
NM-056	nat	Y	2/0	Y	3
NM-063	nat	Y	2/0	Y	3
NM-066	nat	N	1/0	N	0

1–*Nest Substrate* (s) are nat (natural, e.g. cliffs) or mm (manmade, e.g. bridges and buildings). *Occupied* and *Successful* nests either Y = Yes or N = No (definitions in Methods). Adult/Subadult often not recorded, thus one number appears. Number of *Young* listed, or unk if last visit was made with young <28 d old.

FWS ID	Nest Substrate[1]	Occupied?[1]	Adult/Subadult[1]	Successful?[1]	Young[1]
NM-069	nat	Y	2/0	Y	3
NM-071	nat	Y	2/0	Y	3
NM-074	nat	Y	2/0	Y	3
NM-075	nat	Y	2/0	unk	unk
NM-077	nat	Y	2/0	N	0
NM-087	nat	Y	2/0	Y	4
NM-089	nat	Y	2/0	Y	3
NM-090	nat	N	1/0	N	0
NM-092	nat	Y	2/0	N	0
NM-097	nat	Y	2/0	Y	2
NM-099	nat	Y	2/0	N	0
NM-100	nat	N	1/0	N	0
TX	nat	Y	2	Y	1
TX	nat	Y	2	Y	1
TX	nat	Y	2	N	0
TX	nat	Y	2	Y	2

Midwestern/Northeastern Monitoring Region

FWS ID	Nest Substrate[1]	Occupied?[1]	Adult/Subadult[1]	Successful?[1]	Young[1]
IA-2	mm	Y	2	Y	4
IL-7	mm	Y	2	Y	3
IN-10	mm	Y	2	Y	4
IN-3	mm	Y	2	Y	4
IN-6	mm	Y	2	Y	4
IN-7	mm	Y	2	Y	4
IN-8	mm	Y	2	N	0
MI-5	mm	Y	2	Y	4
MI-7	mm	Y	2	N	0
MN-11	mm	Y	2	Y	1
MN-17	mm	Y	2	Y	3
MN-19	mm	Y	2	N	0
MN-21	mm	Y	2	Y	3
MN-27	mm	Y	2	N	0
MN-5	nat	Y	2	unk	unk
MN-9	mm	Y	2	N	0
OH-1	mm	Y	2	Y	2
OH-11	mm	Y	2	Y	1
OH-15	mm	Y	2	Y	3
OH-6	mm	Y	2	N	0
WI-14	mm	Y	2	Y	3
WI-2	mm	Y	2	Y	4
WI-9	mm	N	1	N	0
NH05	nat	Y	2	Y	2
NH06	nat	Y	2	Y	2

1–*Nest Substrate* (s) are nat (natural, e.g. cliffs) or mm (manmade, e.g. bridges and buildings). *Occupied* and *Successful* nests either Y = Yes or N = No (definitions in Methods). Adult/Subadult often not recorded, thus one number appears. Number of *Young* listed, or unk if last visit was made with young <28 d old.

FWS ID	Nest Substrate[1]	Occupied?[1]	Adult/Subadult[1]	Successful?[1]	Young[1]
NH07	nat	Y	2	Y	2
NH11	nat	Y	2	N	0
NH14	nat	Y	2	Y	2
VT5	nat	Y	2	N	0
VT6	nat	Y	2	N	0
VT12	nat	Y	2	Y	3
VT13	nat	N	1	N	0
VT14	nat	Y	2	Y	3
VT15	nat	Y	2	N	0
VT16	nat	Y	2	Y	1
VT17	nat	Y	2	Y	3
VT20	nat	Y	2	N	0
VT22	nat	Y	2	N	0
VT28	nat	Y	2	Y	2
DE04	mm	Y	2	Y	3
MD01	mm	Y	2	Y	4
MD04	mm	Y	2	Y	2
MD05	mm	Y	2	N	0
MD06	mm	Y	2	Y	4
MD07	mm	Y	2	Y	3
MD11	mm	Y	2	Y	3
CT03	nat	N	1	N	0
ME01	nat	Y	2	N	0
ME03	nat	Y	2	Y	2
ME04	nat	Y	2	N	0
ME07	nat	Y	2	Y	3
ME16	nat	N	0	N	0
NY01	nat	Y	2	unk	unk
NY05	nat	N	0	N	0
NY06	nat	Y	2	Y	2
NY08	nat	Y	2	unk	unk
NY10	nat	Y	1	Y	3
NY15	nat	N	0	N	0
NY16	nat	Y	2	Y	3
NY28	nat	Y	2	Y	2
NY30	mm	Y	2	Y	4
NY34	mm	Y	2	N	0
NY35	mm	Y	2	N	0
NY40	mm	Y	2	Y	2
NY41	mm	Y	2	Y	4
NY42	mm	N	0	N	0
NY44	nat	Y	2	Y	1
NY46	mm	Y	2	Y	3

1–*Nest Substrate* (s) are nat (natural, e.g. cliffs) or mm (manmade, e.g. bridges and buildings). *Occupied* and *Successful* nests either Y = Yes or N = No (definitions in Methods). Adult/Subadult often not recorded, thus one number appears. Number of *Young* listed, or unk if last visit was made with young <28 d old.

FWS ID	Nest Substrate[1]	Occupied?[1]	Adult/Subadult[1]	Successful?[1]	Young[1]
NY48	mm	Y	2	Y	3
NY51	nat	Y	2	Y	3
NY53	nat	N	2	N	0
MA01	mm	Y	2	Y	3
MA04	mm	Y	2	Y	1
MA08	mm	Y	2	Y	3
NJ02	mm	Y	2	N	0
NJ06	mm	Y	2	Y	4
NJ07	mm	Y	2	Y	3
NJ09	mm	Y	2	Y	1
NJ12	mm	Y	2	Y	2
NJ14	mm	Y	2	Y	4
NJ19	mm	Y	2	Y	3
NJ21	mm	Y	2	Y	2
PA11	mm	Y	2	Y	2
RI02	mm	Y	2	unk	unk
VA02	mm	Y	2	Y	3
VA05	mm	Y	2	Y	5
VA09	mm	Y	2	Y	2
VA10	mm	Y	2	Y	4
VA14	mm	N	0	N	0
VA17	mm	Y	2	Y	2
VA18	mm	Y	2	N	0
VA22	mm	Y	2	Y	0
VA24	mm	Y	2	Y	3
VA25	mm	Y	2	Y	3
VA26	mm	Y	2	N	0

Southeastern Monitoring Region

FWS ID	Nest Substrate[1]	Occupied?[1]	Adult/Subadult[1]	Successful?[1]	Young[1]
NC1	nat	Y	2/0	N	0
NC2	nat	Y	2/0	Y	3
NC3	nat	Y	2/0	N	0
NC4	nat	Y	2/0	Y	1
NC5	nat	Y	2/0	N	0
NC6	nat	Y	2/0	N	0
NC7	nat	Y	2/0	Y	3
NC8	nat	Y	2/0	Y	2
NC9	nat	Y	2/0	Y	2
NC10	nat	Y	2/0	Y	2
SC1	nat	Y	2/0	unk	unk
KY1	mm	N	1/0	N	0
KY2	mm	Y	?	Y	4
KY3	mm	Y	?	Y	2

1–*Nest Substrate* (s) are nat (natural, e.g. cliffs) or mm (manmade, e.g. bridges and buildings). *Occupied* and *Successful* nests either Y = Yes or N = No (definitions in Methods). Adult/Subadult often not recorded, thus one number appears. Number of *Young* listed, or unk if last visit was made with young <28 d old.

FWS ID	Nest Substrate[1]	Occupied?[1]	Adult/Subadult[1]	Successful?[1]	Young[1]
KY4	mm	Y	2/0	Y	1
KY5	mm	Y	2/0	Y	3
TN1	nat	Y	2/0	unk	unk
TN2	mm	Y	1/1	Y	0
TN3	nat	Y	2/0	Y	2
GA1	mm	Y	2/0	Y	2
GA2	mm	Y	1/?	Y	1

Rocky Mountain/Great Plains Monitoring Region

FWS ID	Nest Substrate[1]	Occupied?[1]	Adult/Subadult[1]	Successful?[1]	Young[1]
CO-02	nat	Y	2/0	Y	2
CO-112	nat	Y	2/0	Y	1
CO-115	nat	N	0	N	0
CO-122	nat	Y	2/0	Y	2
CO-123	nat	N	1/0	N	0
CO-124	nat	Y	2/0	N	0
CO-131	nat	N	0	N	0
CO-132	nat	Y	2/0	Y	2
CO-138	nat	Y	2/0	N	0
CO-147	nat	Y	2/0	unk	unk
CO-149	nat	Y	2/0	Y	3
CO-152	nat	N	1/0	N	0
CO-22	nat	Y	2/0	N	0
CO-32	nat	Y	2/0	Y	2
CO-41	nat	Y	2/0	unk	unk
CO-42	nat	Y	2/0	N	0
CO-43	nat	Y	2/0	N	0
CO-54	nat	Y	2/0	N	0
CO-58	nat	Y	2/0	Y	3
CO-69	nat	Y	1/1	N	0
CO-71	nat	Y	2/0	N	0
CO-75	nat	N	0	N	0
CO-92	nat	Y	2/0	N	0
CO-94	nat	Y	2/0	N	0
CO-97	nat	Y	2/0	N	0
Mt-03	nat	Y	2/0	Y	2
Mt-06	mm	N	0	N	0
Mt-10	nat	N	0	N	0
Mt-11	nat	Y	2/0	Y	2
Mt-12	nat	Y	2/0	Y	4
Mt-17	nat	N	0	N	0
Mt-24	nat	Y	2/0	Y	2
Mt-26	nat	Y	2/0	Y	3
Mt-27	nat	Y	2/0	Y	3

1–*Nest Substrate* (s) are nat (natural, e.g. cliffs) or mm (manmade, e.g. bridges and buildings). *Occupied* and *Successful* nests either Y = Yes or N = No (definitions in Methods). Adult/Subadult often not recorded, thus one number appears. Number of *Young* listed, or unk if last visit was made with young <28 d old.

FWS ID	Nest Substrate[1]	Occupied?[1]	Adult/Subadult[1]	Successful?[1]	Young[1]
Mt-29	nat	Y	2	Y	3
Mt-33	nat	Y	2	Y	3
Mt-34	nat	Y	2	Y	1
Mt-35	nat	Y	2	Y	2
Mt-41	nat	N	0	N	0
Mt-43	nat	N	0	N	0
UT-012	mm	Y	2	Y	1
UT-016	mm	Y	2	N	0
UT-017	mm	Y	2	Y	2
UT-024	nat	Y	2	Y	1
UT-025	nat	Y	1	N	0
UT-027	nat	Y	2	Y	2
UT-029	nat	Y	2	unk	unk
UT-030	nat	Y	2	unk	unk
UT-033	nat	Y	2	N	0
UT-037	nat	Y	2	Y	2
UT-040	nat	Y	2	Y	1
UT-041	nat	Y	2	Y	1
UT-046	nat	Y	2	N	0
UT-047	nat	Y	2	Y	2
UT-064	nat	Y	2	unk	unk
UT-072	nat	Y	2	unk	unk
UT-081	nat	Y	2	Y	3
UT-090	nat	Y	2	Y	2
UT-098	nat	Y	1	Y	2
UT-099	nat	Y	2	Y	1
UT-100	nat	N	0	N	0
UT-105	nat	Y	2	Y	1
UT-118	nat	Y	2	Y	2
UT-124	nat	Y	2	unk	unk
UT-127	nat	Y	2	Y	1
UT-129	nat	Y	2	Y	2
UT-131	nat	Y	2	unk	unk
UT-135	nat	Y	2	Y	2
UT-136	nat	Y	2	Y	2
UT-144	nat	Y	2	Y	1
UT-162	nat	Y	2	Y	2
UT-163	nat	Y	2	Y	1
UT-172	nat	N	0	N	0
UT-177	nat	Y	2	Y	2
UT-181	nat	Y	2	N	0
WY-2	nat	Y	2	Y	2
WY-10	nat	Y	2	Y	2

1–*Nest Substrate* (s) are nat (natural, e.g. cliffs) or mm (manmade, e.g. bridges and buildings). *Occupied* and *Successful* nests either Y = Yes or N = No (definitions in Methods). Adult/Subadult often not recorded, thus one number appears. Number of *Young* listed, or unk if last visit was made with young <28 d old.

FWS ID	Nest Substrate[1]	Occupied?[1]	Adult/Subadult[1]	Successful?[1]	Young[1]
WY-12	nat	Y	2	Y	3
WY-14	nat	Y	2	Y	2
WY-20	nat	Y	2	Y	2
WY-23	nat	Y	2	Y	2
WY-24	nat	Y	2	N	0
WY-25	nat	Y	2	Y	2
WY-27	nat	Y	2	Y	2
WY-32	nat	Y	2	Y	3
WY-33	nat	Y	2	Y	4
WY-42	nat	Y	1	N	0
WY-45	nat	Y	2	Y	1
WY-60	nat	Y	2	Y	1
WY-61	nat	Y	2	Y	2

Interior Alaska Monitoring Region

Yukon River km

	Nest Substrate[1]	Occupied?[1]	Adult/Subadult[1]	Successful?[1]	Young[1]
3	nat	Y	2	Y	2
9.5	nat	Y	2	N	0
14	nat	Y	2	Y	2
20	nat	Y	2	Y	2
26	nat	Y	2	Y	3
31.5	nat	Y	2	Y	2
38	nat	Y	2	N	0
45	nat	Y	2	N	0
48.5	nat	Y	2	Y	3
51.5	nat	Y	2	N	0
56	nat	Y	2	Y	2
57.5	nat	Y	2	N	0
73.5	nat	Y	2	N	0
76.5	nat	Y	2	Y	4
82.5	nat	Y	2	N	0
88	nat	Y	2	Y	3
90.5	nat	Y	3	Y	3
95.5	nat	Y	2	N	0
112	nat	Y	2	Y	1
117	nat	Y	3	Y	2
123_0	nat	Y	2	N	0
124	nat	Y	2	Y	2
128	nat	Y	3	N	0
138	nat	Y	2	Y	3
141.5	nat	Y	2	Y	1
149.5	nat	Y	2	Y	3
154	nat	Y	2	Y	3

1–*Nest Substrate* (s) are nat (natural, e.g. cliffs) or mm (manmade, e.g. bridges and buildings). *Occupied* and *Successful* nests either Y = Yes or N = No (definitions in Methods). Adult/Subadult often not recorded, thus one number appears. Number of *Young* listed, or unk if last visit was made with young <28 d old.

FWS ID	Nest Substrate[1]	Occupied?[1]	Adult/Subadult[1]	Successful?[1]	Young[1]
180	nat	Y	2	Y	2
184	nat	Y	2	N	0
187	nat	Y	2	Y	2
191.5	nat	Y	2	N	0
195	nat	Y	2	Y	2
196.6	nat	Y	2	N	0
197	nat	Y	2	N	0
199	nat	Y	2	Y	3
200.5	nat	Y	4	Y	2
205	nat	Y	2	N	0
208.5	nat	Y	2	N	0
210.5	nat	Y	2	N	0
211.5	nat	Y	2	N	0
224.5	nat	Y	2	Y	3
229	nat	Y	2	N	0
233	nat	Y	2	Y	2
235	nat	Y	2	N	0
239.5	nat	Y	2	Y	2
243.2	nat	Y	2	N	0
248.5	nat	Y	2	Y	2
254	nat	Y	2	Y	1
Tanana River km					
96.5	nat	Y	2	Y	2
103	nat	Y	2	Y	1
130	nat	Y	2	N	0
135	nat	Y	2	Y	4
181	nat	Y	2	Y	3
188	nat	Y	2	N	0
205	nat	Y	2	Y	4
211	nat	N	1	N	0
214	nat	N	0	N	0
221.5	nat	Y	2	Y	4
243	nat	Y	2	Y	4
244.5	nat	Y	2	Y	2
246	nat	N	0	N	0
247	nat	N	0	N	0
248	nat	Y	2	Y	4
257	nat	Y	2	Y	2
258.5	nat	Y	2	Y	2
269.5	nat	Y	2	N	0
273	nat	Y	2	Y	3
280.5	nat	Y	2	Y	1

1–*Nest Substrate* (s) are nat (natural, e.g. cliffs) or mm (manmade, e.g. bridges and buildings). *Occupied* and *Successful* nests either Y = Yes or N = No (definitions in Methods). Adult/Subadult often not recorded, thus one number appears. Number of *Young* listed, or unk if last visit was made with young <28 d old.

FWS ID	Nest Substrate[1]	Occupied?[1]	Adult/Subadult[1]	Successful?[1]	Young[1]
281.5	nat	N	0	N	0
283.5	nat	Y	2	Y	2
288.5	nat	N	0	N	0
299	nat	Y	2	N	0
320	nat	Y	2	Y	4
323	nat	Y	2	N	0
335	nat	N	0	N	0
337.5	nat	Y	2	Y	1
371	nat	Y	2	Y	4
376	nat	Y	2	N	0
380	nat	Y	2	Y	1
386	nat	Y	2	Y	1
405	nat	Y	2	Y	3
408	nat	N	0	N	0
411	nat	Y	2	Y	2
412	nat	Y	2	Y	2
414.5	nat	N	1	N	0
427	nat	Y	2	Y	1
431	nat	Y	2	N	0
436.5	nat	Y	2	N	0
438.5	nat	Y	2	Y	3
443	nat	Y	2	N	0
449	nat	Y	2	N	0
459.5	nat	Y	2	Y	1
470.5	nat	Y	2	Y	2
544.5	nat	N	1	N	0
550.5	nat	Y	2	Y	3
551.5	nat	Y	2	Y	1
578	nat	Y	2	Y	2
586	nat	Y	2	Y	2
610	nat	N	1	N	0
613	nat	Y	2	N	0

1–*Nest Substrate* (s) are nat (natural, e.g. cliffs) or mm (manmade, e.g. bridges and buildings). *Occupied* and *Successful* nests either Y = Yes or N = No (definitions in Methods). Adult/Subadult often not recorded, thus one number appears. Number of *Young* listed, or unk if last visit was made with young <28 d old.

U.S. Department of the Interior
U.S. Fish & Wildlife Service
Route 1, Box 166
Sheperdstown, WV 25443

http://www.fws.gov

March 2006